Earth's Amazing Cycles

Rocks

Jillian Powell
& Kay Coenen

Enslow PUBLISHING

Published in 2026 by Enslow Publishing, LLC
2544 Clinton Street
Buffalo, NY 14224

First published in Great Britain in 2022 by Hodder & Stoughton

The text in this book was previously published in the series "Earth Cycles".

Credits
Series editor: Julia Bird
Designer/Illustrator: Kay Coenen

Manufactured in the United States of America

CPSIA compliance information: Batch #CSENS26: For further information contact Enslow Publishing LLC, New York, New York at 1-800-398-2504.

Please visit our website, www.enslowpublishing.com. For a free color catalog of all our high-quality books, call toll free 1-800-398-2504 or fax 1-877-980-4454.

Cataloging-in-Publication Data
Names: Powell, Jillian, author. | Coenen, Kay, illustrator.
Title: Rocks / Jillian Powell and Kay Coenen.
Description: Buffalo, NY : Enslow Publishing, 2026. | Series: Earth's amazing cycles | Includes glossary and index.
Identifiers: ISBN 9781978544932 (pbk.) | ISBN 9781978544949 (library bound) | ISBN 9781978544956 (ebook)
Subjects: LCSH: Rocks--Juvenile literature. | Petrology--Juvenile literature. | Geochemical cycles--Juvenile literature.
Classification: LCC QE432.2 P694 2026 | DDC 552--dc23

Find us on

Contents

What Are Rocks?

The ground beneath our feet is the surface of the earth's outer layer or crust. This layer is made up entirely of rocks. Most rocks are hard and they come in a range of colors from white through to green and black.

Minerals

Rocks are made of substances called minerals that occur naturally in the ground. Some rocks are made up of a single mineral, such as limestone, which contains calcium carbonate. Others are made up of several minerals, for example granite contains quartz, feldspar, and biotite.

Rock groups

Rocks are placed in three groups, according to how they were formed. These groups are igneous, sedimentary, and metamorphic rocks. Igneous rocks are made from magma, a hot liquid rock found deep in the earth's crust. Sedimentary rocks are made from particles, such as sand and broken shells. Metamorphic rocks are made when other rocks change their form (see pages 20–21).

These rock formations are found in Arizona. They are made from sedimentary rocks, including sandstone and shale.

Oldest and youngest rocks

The oldest rocks in the world are found in northwest Canada. They are metamorphic rocks formed more than 4 billion years ago. The oldest sedimentary rocks are about 3.8 billion years old and are found in southwestern Greenland. The youngest rocks are those which have only just formed. These include igneous rocks made from the lava produced by volcanoes, such as those found on the island of Sicily, from the eruptions of Mount Etna.

Granite is an igneous rock.

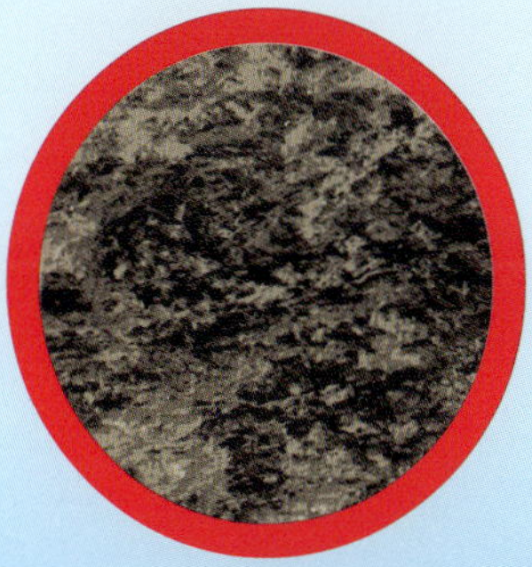

Limestone is a sedimentary rock.

Marble is a metamorphic rock.

Q and A

Q What is the most common mineral on Earth?

A Quartz. This is a mineral that is made of silicon dioxide. Sand is made from quartz and is used to make glass, concrete, and china. Large crystals of quartz are used as gemstones.

Rose- colored quartz is used in jewellery.

Inside the Earth

Amazingly, the ground beneath our feet is moving. You cannot feel it, but it is moving all the time. The surface of the Earth is formed from a layer called the crust. Beneath the crust are two other layers, the mantle and the core.

Red-hot core

The core is at the center of the Earth. Here, temperatures can reach up to 10,800°F (6,000°C). The inner core is a solid ball of metal, mostly iron and nickel. The outer core is made of liquid rock.

The mantle

The Earth's middle layer, the mantle, is about 1,802 miles (2,900 km) thick and is made up of rock. In some places, the rock is so hot that it melts and becomes liquid, like a thick soup. This is called magma. Currents of magma rise up through the mantle to the crust, where they cool and then sink again.

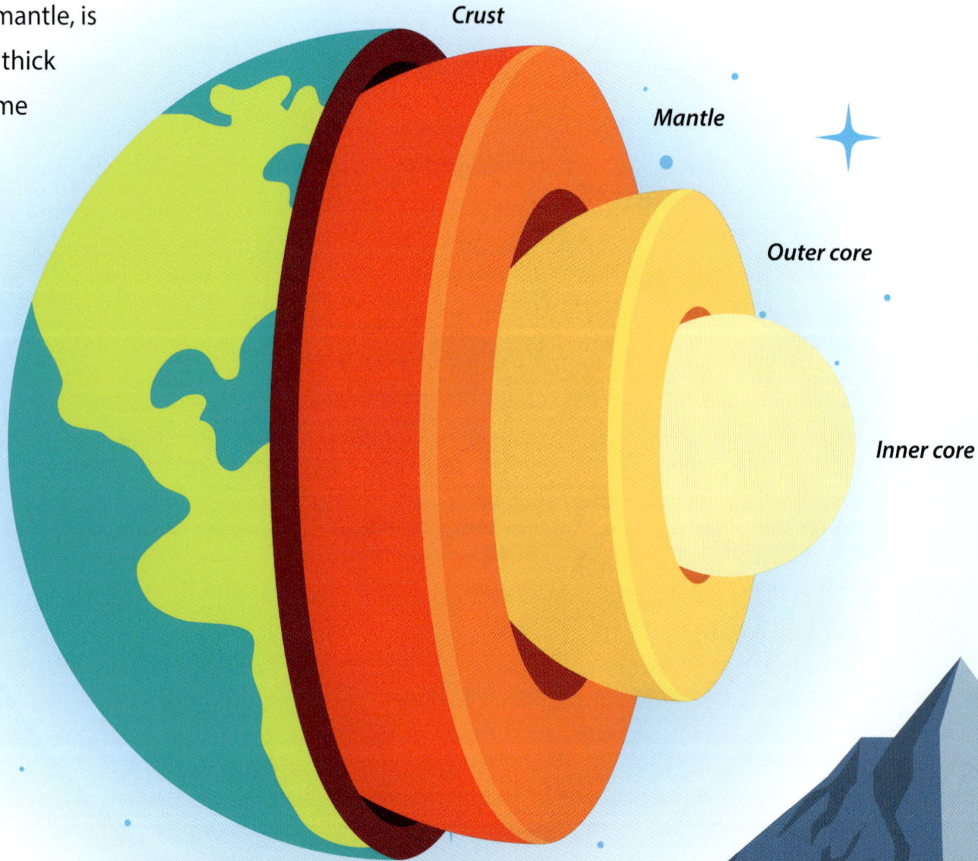

Earth's inner core is solid because the layers above it place huge pressure on it, making the metal turn solid.

The crust

Earth's outer layer, or crust, is made up of large plates that float on the mantle. The plates that make up the land are typically between 22 to 62 miles (35 to 100 km) thick, while oceanic plates are thinner, usually between 3 to 6 miles (5 to 10 km) thick. Currents inside the mantle cause the plates to move. As a result, some plates are colliding, while others are pulling away from each other.

Q and A

Q What is the "Ring of Fire"?

A This is the circle of volcanoes that occur around the Pacific Ocean. Movements of the Pacific plate against neighboring plates produce earthquakes and volcanoes in this region.

The Ring of Fire surrounds the Pacific Ocean.

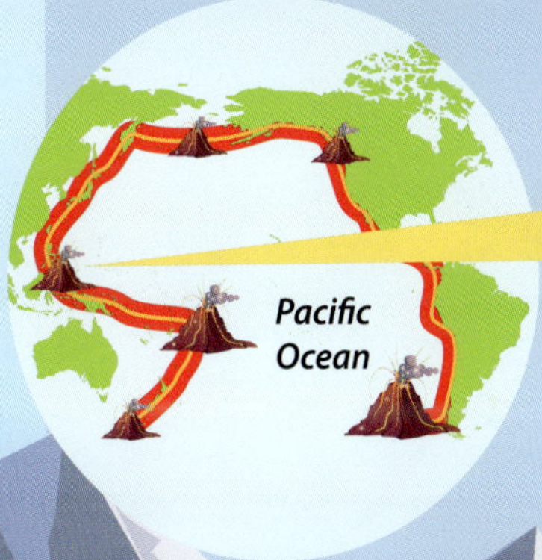

Many active volcanoes are found in the Ring of Fire.

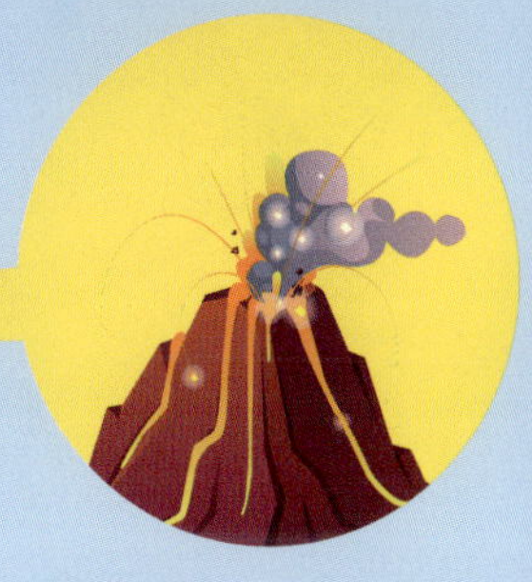

Mountains form when two plates push against each other causing the rocks to crumple and forcing them up.

The Rock Cycle

The rock cycle is a series of changes in which rocks are formed, broken down, and changed into other rocks. The starting point is magma that forms in the mantle. Cracks in the crust allow some of the magma to escape to the surface where it becomes lava and then igneous rock.

3

Lava quickly cools and turns into black igneous rock.

The igneous cycle

Most of the magma cools underground to become igneous rock.

Movements in the crust push the igneous rocks down into the mantle where they melt and become magma again.

2

A volcano forms where lava erupts from the ground.

Sometimes, heat and pressure in the ground cause igneous and sedimentary rock to change into metamorphic rock.

Cycles within cycles

There are mini cycles within the rock cycle called the igneous and sedimentary rock cycles. Also, igneous and sedimentary rocks can both be changed into metamorphic rocks.

1

7

4

Rock particles are carried by rivers into the oceans where they sink to the sea bed. Layers of sediment build up and become sedimentary rock.

5

Eventually, the rock particles become new sedimentary rocks.

The sedimentary cycle

6

Sedimentary rocks at the surface are broken up by the action of wind, rain, and sun.

Q and A

Q How long is the rock cycle?

A The rock cycle takes place over millions of years. Sedimentary rocks, for example, are formed from particles which built up over hundreds of millions of years. Igneous rocks are formed from magma which can take thousands or sometimes millions of years to cool. Later, some of these rocks are changed into metamorphic rocks.

Volcanoes

A volcanic eruption occurs when lava, together with ash and gas, erupts at the earth's surface. Sometimes the volcanic eruption is violent and lava is thrown high into the air. Other eruptions are less violent and lava just oozes out of cracks in the ground. The lava then cools and turns into a solid rock called basalt.

Volcano shapes

Volcanoes are made from layers of lava that have built up over many eruptions. The shape of a volcano depends on the type of lava. Runny lava forms a low, gently sloping shape, like the volcanoes found on the island of Hawaii. These are called shield volcanoes. Thick, sticky lava does not flow easily, so it forms a cone-shaped volcano. Mount Fuji in Japan is a cone-shaped volcano.

Magma is a thick liquid that contains gases and fragments of rock. It collects inside the volcano before it erupts.

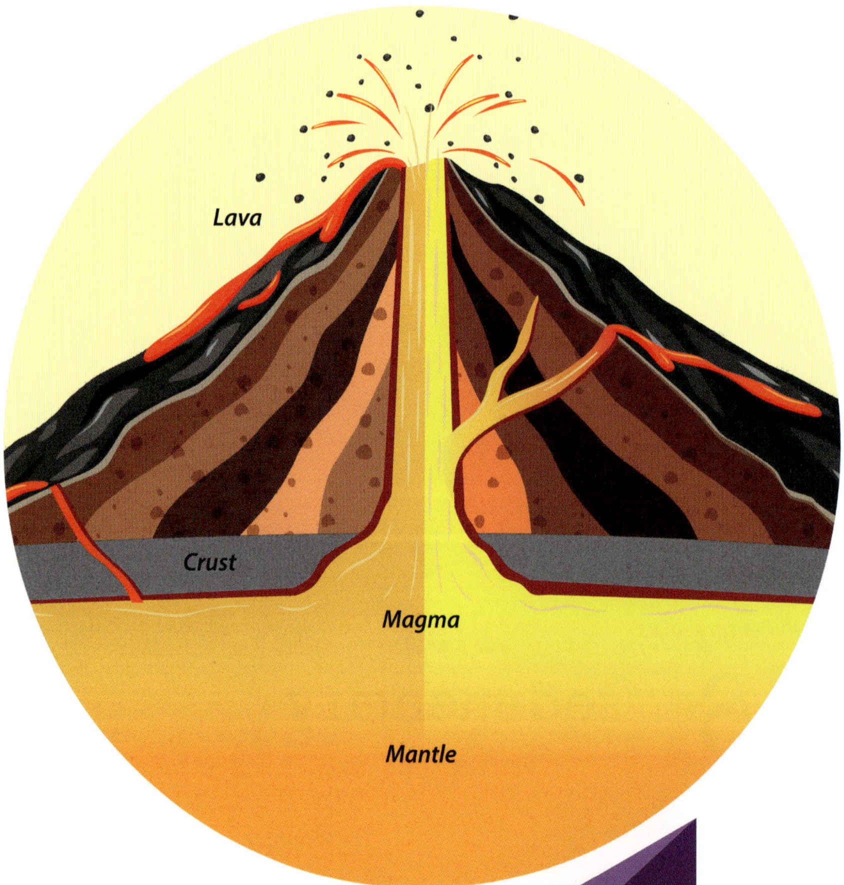

Active or extinct?

Active volcanoes are those that have erupted during the last few thousand years, for example Mount Etna in Sicily and Mount Teide in Tenerife. An extinct volcano is one that has not erupted during the last few thousand to 10,000 years.

Underwater volcanoes

There are around 1,500 active volcanoes on Earth, and most of them are found under the seas and oceans, such as Kolumbo near the Greek island of Santorini in the Mediterranean. The cone of this volcano suddenly appeared above the water in 1650, and the eruption killed 70 islanders.

Q and A

Q What is a caldera?

A This is a huge crater that forms when the top of the volcano collapses either during or after an eruption. Sometimes it fills with water to form a crater lake.

A crater lake

Making Igneous Rocks

Only a small fraction of the Earth's magma rises to the surface and escapes as lava. Most remains underground, where it cools to form igneous rocks.

Cooling underground

Magma moves towards the Earth's surface through cracks in the crust. Eventually, the cracks stop and the magma is trapped. The hot magma cools very slowly and becomes solid rock.

These mountains are formed from granite, a type of igneous rock.

Crystals

Crystals form as the magma cools. The size of the crystals depends on how quickly it cools. Large crystals form when the magma cools very slowly, such as the crystals in gabbro and granite. Fast cooling produces small crystals, like the crystals in the rock basalt.

Q and A

Q What is a geyser?

A A geyser is a jet of hot water and steam that spurts from the ground. The water is heated by hot rocks below the earth's surface. Old Faithful in Yellowstone National Park is one of the most well-known geysers in the world. It erupts every 60 to 90 minutes, sending thousands of gallons of hot water into the air.

Hot rocks

In some parts of the world, hot igneous rocks lie close to the Earth's surface. The rocks heat water in the ground and wells can be dug to reach it. In other places, hot water bubbles out of the ground forming geysers and hot water pools, which can be used to produce electricity.

Rocks Under Water

Rivers carry a lot of sediment, such as sand, silt and clay, that has been washed into the water. These particles are the raw materials for new sedimentary rocks.

Mud on the sea bed

The sediment carried by rivers ends up in the sea, where it drops to the sea bed. Beneath the surface of the sea bed are many layers of sediment that have built up over millions of years. As more and more sediment lands on the sea bed, the lower layers get squashed. The weight pushing down on the sediment causes the water to be squeezed out. When this happens, salts in the sediment form crystals. The salt crystals help to glue the particles together and form sedimentary rock.

Mudflats on a river estuary at low tide. Some of the mud will be washed into the ocean where it will sink to the sea bed.

These rocks are formed from limestone, a type of sedimentary rock. The rocks have been broken up by the waves, forming stacks.

Clues in rocks

Sedimentary rocks form over hundreds of millions of years, and during this time the sediments change because of variations in climate and vegetation. This means a sequence of different sedimentary rocks is formed. Geologists can study the sequence of rocks in a cliff to find out about the earth's climate millions of years ago.

The cliffs of the Grand Canyon are made up of layers of sedimentary rock, including sandstone and mudstone. The rocks are the top are about 270 million years old, while those at the bottom are believed to have formed around 1.8 billion years ago.

Q and A

Q How do rocks tells us what happened to the dinosaurs?

A Scientists believe that a huge meteor hit the earth, wiping out many plant and animal species, including the dinosaurs. By testing sedimentary rocks for iridium, a substance found in meteors, scientists have proved that a huge meteor hit the Earth about 65 million years ago.

Sedimentary Rocks

There are many different types of sedimentary rock. They vary because of the different types of particle from which they are made.

Limestone

Limestone rocks are rich in a mineral called calcite, which contains calcium carbonate. This is because they are made up mostly of the crushed shells of sea animals, such as mollusks, that died millions of years ago. Chalk is one type of limestone. It is made from the skeletons of tiny animals too small to be seen with the human eye.

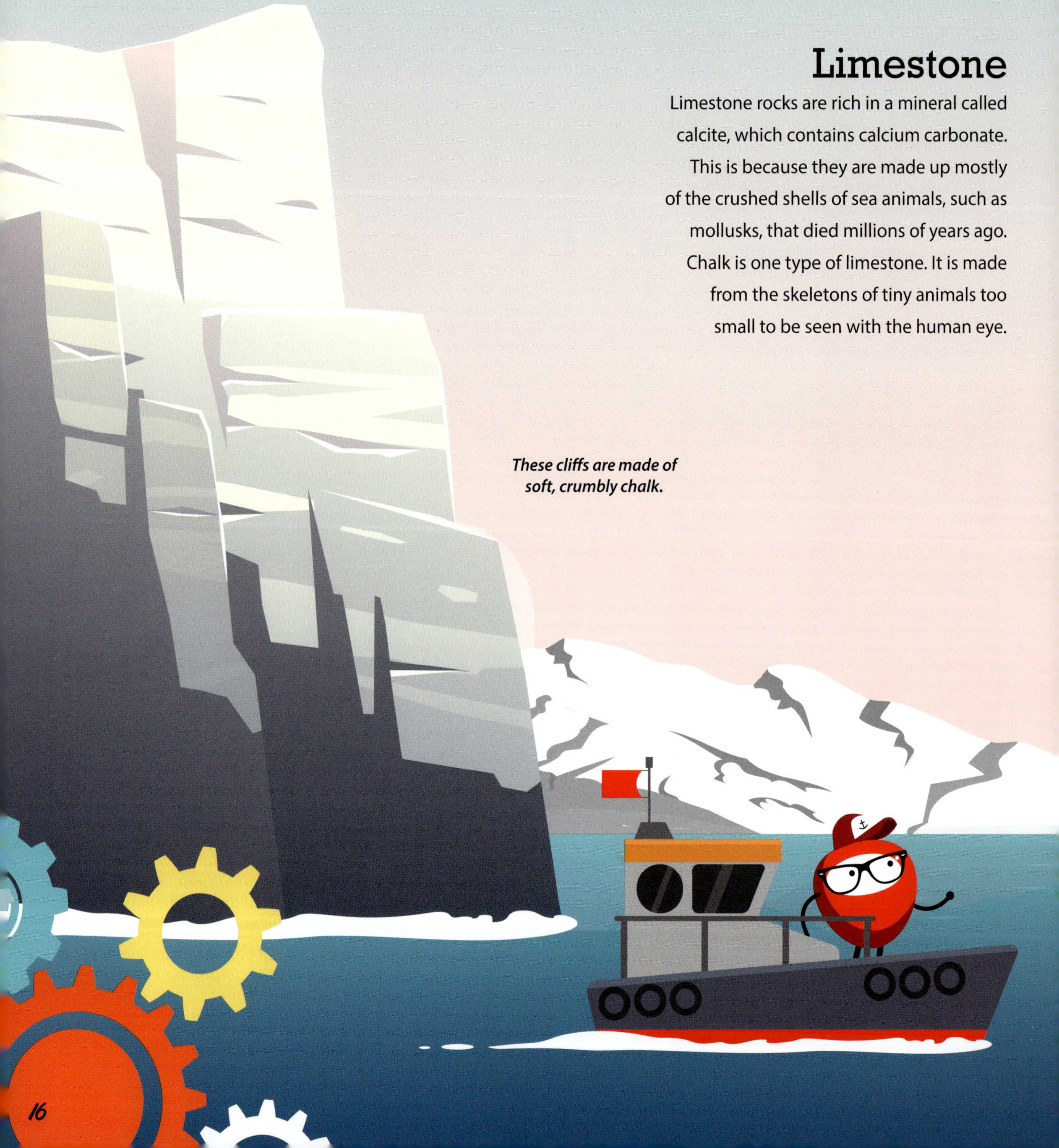

These cliffs are made of soft, crumbly chalk.

Sandstone

Sandstone is made from grains of sand. A grain of sand is made of quartz (see page 5), a common mineral. The grains are stuck together by a different mineral called silica.

Conglomerate

Conglomerate is a lumpy rock made up of stones, pebbles, and gravel that have become glued together by silica or calcium carbonate. Conglomerates are often found along beaches and rivers.

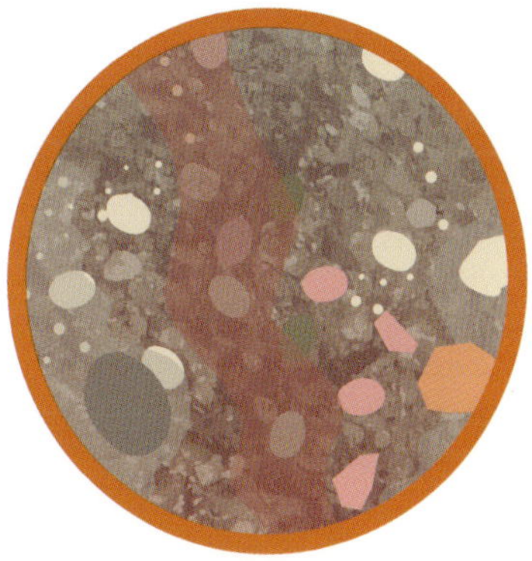

Shale

Shale is a soft rock made from fine grains of clay. It is the most common sedimentary rock and is found around the world. It is used in brick-making and construction.

Q and A

Q What is a fossil?

A A fossil is the preserved remains of an animal or plant in a rock.
A fossil forms when the remains of an animal drop to the bottom of a lake or ocean and the soft parts of the body are broken down. The hard parts, such as bones or shell, become covered in mud and sand and eventually become part of the rock.

Folding and Faulting

The plates that make up the earth's crust are moving all the time. When this happens, the rocks along the edges of the crust become stretched and squeezed.

Folds

When the plates move, some of the rocks are pushed up and the layers, instead of lying horizontally, are pushed upwards or even become folded.

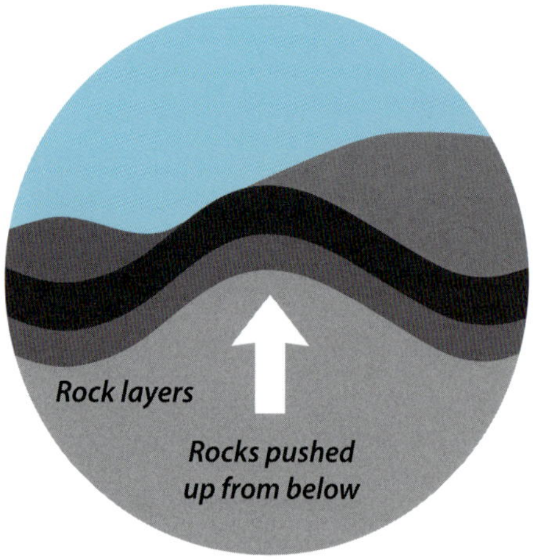

Folds form when rocks are pushed upwards by movements in the earth's crust.

These rocks made from mudstone and shale have been pushed so that the layers are almost vertical.

Faults

The forces that move the earth's plates are so powerful that huge masses of rock can split and move apart. Imagine you are trying to break a pencil. First, you apply a lot of force with both hands and the pencil bends. Then, the pencil snaps in the middle. This happens in rocks. Great pressure is applied, and suddenly the rocks break and slide past each other. This is called shearing and it creates a fault, or break, in the rock.

The Rift Valley in Africa was formed when two faults appeared in the rock. The block of rock in the middle dropped to create a deep valley.

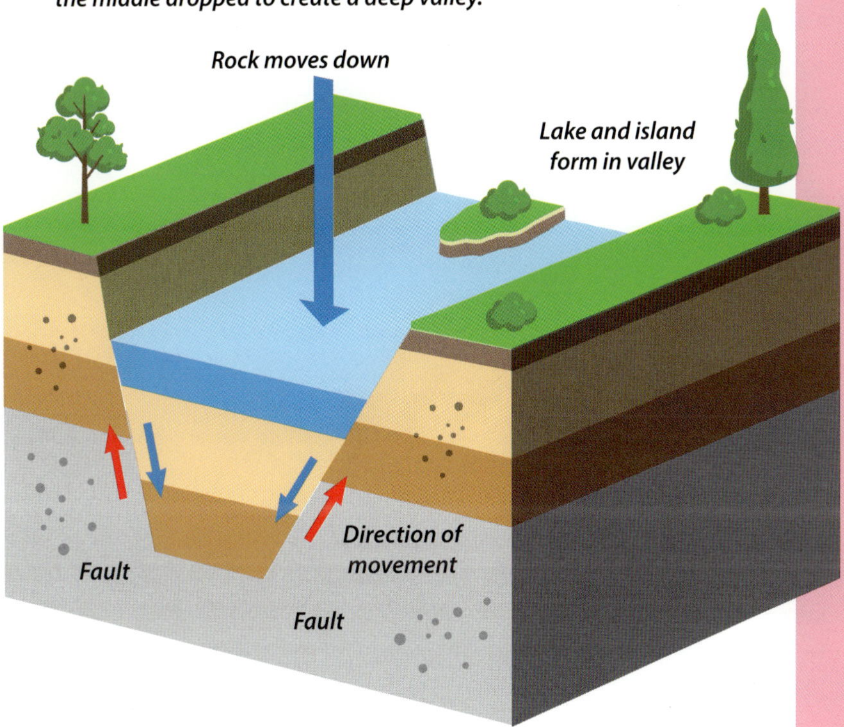

Mountain building

When two plates push against each other, the rocks crumple and are pushed upwards to form mountains. The Himalayas were formed over millions of years when the Indian plate collided with the Asiatic plate. These movements are still taking place, so the Himalayas are growing taller each year.

Q and A

Q What causes earthquakes?

A An earthquake occurs when two plates suddenly slide past each other, causing a release of energy and a shock wave that shakes the ground. Most earthquakes are too small to be noticed, but a major earthquake can cause huge damage and loss of life.

Re-made Rocks

The extreme heat and pressure that exist far beneath the Earth's surface can change the structure and appearance of rocks. This creates metamorphic rocks such as gneiss and marble.

Crushed and squeezed

Rocks can also be changed by crushing and squeezing, processes that take place deep in the ground over several million years. Even the shape of the particles can be altered, from round to almost flat. Both igneous and sedimentary rocks can change form when placed under pressure. When sandstone is changed to quartzite for example, the layers disappear and the crystals melt and reform.

Granite can be changed into the metamorphic rock gneiss. Gneiss consists of alternating bands of dark and light minerals.

Gneiss has been used to build structures for thousands of years, such as this prehistoric stone circle.

Q and A

Q What is slate?

A Slate is a layered metamorphic rock that is made from shale (see page 17). The layers split apart easily, and form thin sheets that can be used for roof tiles.

Marble

High temperatures and pressure can change limestone into marble. Marble is a popular building material because when it's shined, it has a shiny, hard surface. It is a harder rock than limestone, but not as hard as granite. There are many different types of marble, each named after the place where it is found. Some of the best-quality marble comes from Carrara in Italy.

The Leaning Tower of Pisa is built of white Carrara marble.

Weathered Rocks

Rocks do not remain the same for ever. When they are exposed to the weather (the sun, rain, and wind) they start to change. This is called weathering.

Sun and wind

Rocks in the desert become very hot during the day and expand. At night, temperatures fall and the rocks shrink again. This constant expansion and contraction causes thin layers of rock to peel away from the surface. This is a form of physical weathering. Wind can also wear away the surface of a rock.

When sandstone is weathered by the wind, it can form spectacular swirling shapes.

Freeze and thaw

Freeze-thaw weathering occurs in places where water freezes. Water trickles through cracks in the rocks, and freezes on cold nights. Water expands as it freezes and the force of the expanding ice causes the cracks to become larger. Then the ice thaws (melts) and the water can go even further into the rock. Eventually, the rock breaks apart.

Rain and weathering

Rain simply falling on to the surface of some rocks can gradually wear away the surface. This is because rainwater is not pure water. It contains substances such as weak acids. When rainwater falls onto limestone and chalk rocks, the acid reacts with the calcium carbonate and slowly wears away the surface. This is known as chemical weathering.

This narrow passageway has been formed by torrents of water wearing away the rock.

Q and A

Q How does a rock arch form?

A A rock arch is formed by the process of weathering. The wind blows sand over the surface of rocks, and wears away the softer rocks. This leaves behind the harder rocks. One of the best-known rock arches is Delicate Arch in Utah. It is made from sandstone and is one of more than 2,000 natural arches in Arches National Park.

Rock arch

Erosion

Once a rock has been weathered into small pieces, the pieces may be moved to another place by the wind or water. This is called erosion.

Erosion often takes place at the same time as weathering. Weathering produces the small pieces of rock that are carried away or eroded by wind and water. This exposes fresh rock to be weathered.

Retreating cliffs

Cliffs along the coasts are constantly battered by the sea, especially during storms. The force of the waves smashes rocks against cliffs, wearing away the rock at the bottom. Eventually, so much rock has been removed from the bottom that the rest of the cliff collapses. Cliffs made of soft rocks, such as clay, retreat more quickly than those made of harder rocks.

These cliffs are formed from soft chalk rock, which is being worn away by the waves.

Sandy beaches

Swirling sea water grinds smaller pieces of rocks together, so they become smaller and rounder, creating pebbles and eventually sand. When the waves retreat back down the beach, they carry the pebbles and sand away. The sand and pebbles are dropped further along the coast where they form beaches. Depending on the tides, some beaches gain sand from elsewhere, while others continually lose their sand.

Sand is carried along this coast by the tides. The bar of sand is getting longer as more sand is added to the end.

Q and A

Q What is a groin?

A A groin is a narrow barrier which extends down the beach into the sea to stop the tide carrying away sand and pebbles. It is built from materials such as rock, wood, or concrete. Groins are part of the coastal defenses built along coastlines that are at risk of erosion.

The groins on this beach prevent the sand from being carried away with the tide.

Soil

Soil covers much of the surface of the land.
It is made of particles of weathered rock mixed with organic material, such as dead leaves.

Plant roots grow through soil and take up water and nutrients from it.

Sand, silt, and clay

Soil contains a mix of sand, silt, and clay. Sand is the largest of the three particles. These particles come from the weathering of rocks. A clay soil does not allow water to drain easily through it. In contrast, a sandy soil allows water to drain easily, but the soil dries up in summer. Loam has a good mix of sand, silt, and clay and this creates a soil that is good for growing crops.

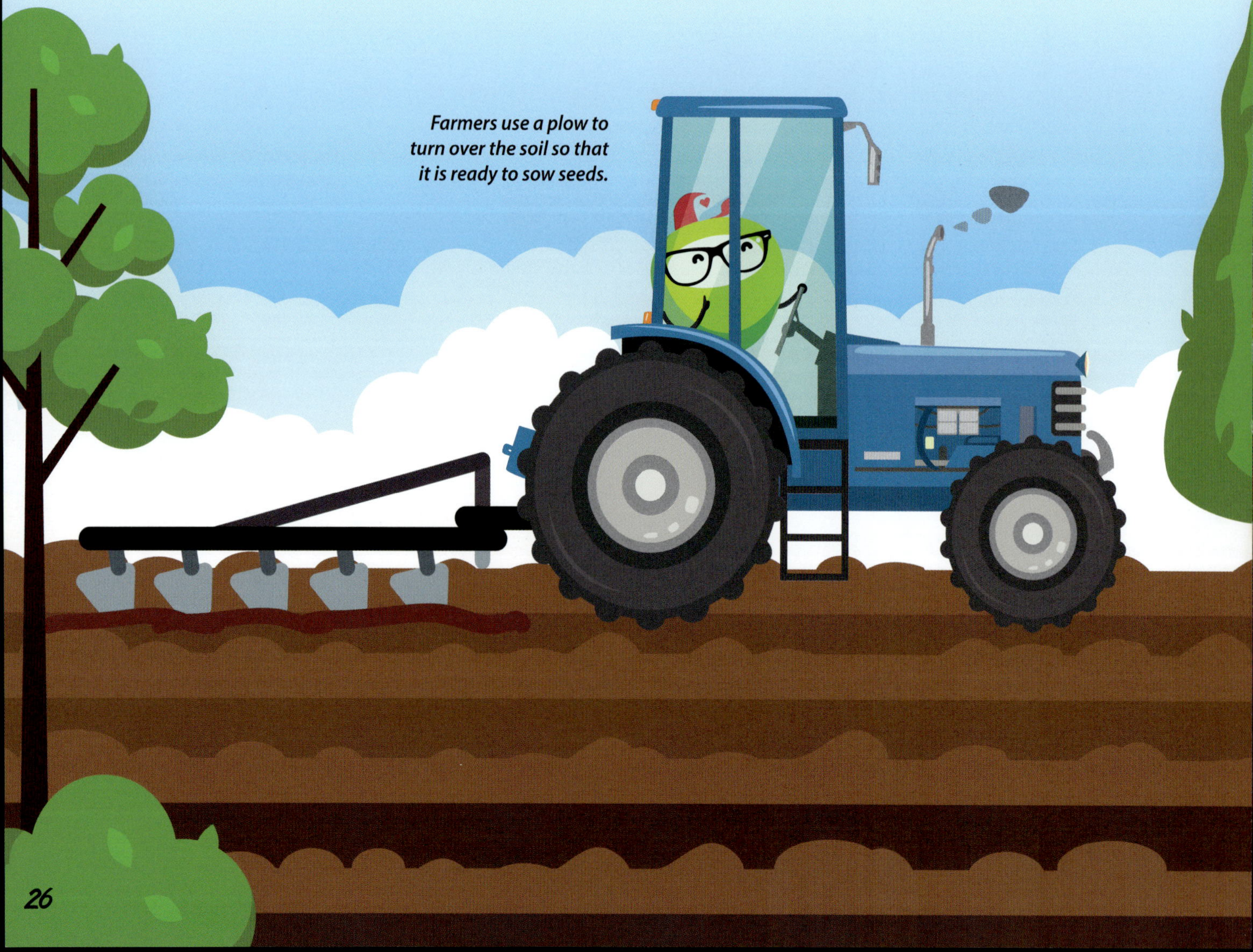

Farmers use a plow to turn over the soil so that it is ready to sow seeds.

Humus

Fallen leaves and other parts of plants break down to form a substance called humus. Humus is good for the soil. It helps to improve the drainage, makes the soil easier to work and provides nutrients to the plants.

Soil erosion

Soil needs protection from the weather. This is usually provided by plants as their roots hold the soil together. However, if the plants are removed, the soil is exposed to the weather. Then the soil may be washed or blown away.

Water has washed away the soil beneath this tree, leaving the roots exposed.

Q and A

Q What is a soil profile?

A This is a vertical cut made down through the soil to the rock, which reveals all the different layers that make up the soil. A good, loamy soil used for farming will extend deep into the ground, but some soils are really thin, such as those that occur over chalk.

The spade shows the depth of this soil.

Rocks and People

Rocks are an important part of the earth's landscape, creating mountains and cliffs and many other features. They also have many uses. They can be dug, or mined, from the ground in huge quarries, and used to create buildings, roads, and even jewelry. However, rocks can be damaged by the activities of people.

Tourism

Mountains and rocky landscapes are popular tourist attractions. However, too many tourists can lead to damage to the surfaces of rocks.

Acid rain

Acid rain is a form of air pollution and it can damage rock (see page 23). Rain is naturally slightly acidic, but pollution from cars and industry increases its acidity. When acid rain falls on buildings made from soft rocks such as limestone, it causes more weathering. This damage is worldwide and can be seen on cathedrals and castles in Europe, in the Parthenon in Athens, Greece and the pyramids in Egypt.

Q and A

Q Is air pollution damaging the Taj Mahal?

A Yes. The Taj Mahal in India is built from strong white marble, but air pollution from heavy traffic and nearby industry is damaging it. Cracks are appearing in the walls and the white marble has dirty stains. The Indian government is working to improve air quality and to save this great building from further damage.

The Parthenon has been badly damaged by air pollution created by the heavy traffic in Athens.

Glossary

acidic containing acid

acid rain rain that is more acidic than normal due to the presence of weak acids; a type of air pollution produced by burning coal and oil, which damages rocks

active volcano a volcano that has erupted in the last 10,000 years

arch a curved shape, like an upside-down U

ash particles of rock thrown out during a volcanic eruption

basalt an igneous rock, usually formed when lava cools and becomes solid

biotite a dark mineral found in igneous and metamorphic rocks

calcite a type of mineral made of calcium carbonate, found in limestone, chalk, and marble

chemical weathering the breakdown of rocks caused by the substances found in rainwater, such as acids

climate the regular pattern of weather experienced in a particular place over a long period of time

collide to crash together

cone-shaped volcano a volcano with tapering sides that form a point

contract to become shallower or smaller

core the center of the Earth

crater a bowl-shaped hole or opening at the top of a volcano

crust the outer layer of the Earth

crystal a solid formed when a liquid cools, often having a shiny appearance

current the flow of liquid in a particular direction

erosion the wearing away of rock by wind and water

eruption the release of lava and ash from a volcano

expand to increase in size or volume

extinct volcano a volcano that has not erupted during the last 10,000 years

fault a large crack or break through a mass of rock

feldspar a common mineral containing silicon, found in igneous rocks. When it is weathered it forms clays

folded a bend in a layer of rocks

fossil the preserved remains of prehistoric animals and plants

geologist a person who studies rocks

gneiss a metamorphic rock, formed from granite

granite a type of igneous rock with large crystals of quartz, which is widely used for building

humus organic matter, such as decayed leaves, that forms part of the soil

igneous rock a type of rock formed from magma when it cools and becomes solid

lava the liquid rock, called magma, that erupts from volcanoes

limestone a type of sedimentary rock

loam a type of soil

magma liquid rock beneath the Earth's surface

mantle the thick layer of hot rock beneath the Earth's crust

meteors lumps of rocks that enter the Earth's atmosphere from space

metamorphic rock rocks that have undergone change

mineral a natural substance in the ground

nickel a metal with a silvery appearance

nutrient a substance needed by plants and animals for healthy growth; plants get their nutrients from the soil

oceanic plates parts of the Earth's crust under the oceans

organic material matter that was once living, for example dead leaves

particle a tiny piece of rock

physical weathering the breakdown of rocks by the sun, wind and water

plate part of the earth's crust

pressure a pushing force on a surface, such as the weight of rocks near the surface pushing down on rocks below

quarry a place where rocks are dug from the ground

quartz a type of mineral

sediment particles of sand, silt, and clay that are carried by water and which settle on the bed of a river, lake or ocean

sedimentary rock rock made from layers of sediment

shearing when two huge blocks of rock slide past each other

shield volcano a volcano with a shallow or low shape

shock wave a vibration that travels through the ground after an earthquake or volcanic eruption

silica a glass-like substance found in magma

silt small particles of sand

stack a steep column of rock in the sea found near a coast. It is created when the rocks of a cliff are eroded, leaving just the stack.

tides the daily rise and fall of the sea along the coast

weathering the breaking down of rocks when they are exposed to the weather

Index

Further reading

Do-It-Again Rock Cycle: Rex Ruby (Bearport Publishing Company, 2025)

Geology Rocks series by Izzi Howell & Claudia Martin (Wayland, 2023)

Step Into Science: Rocks & Soil by Peter Riley (Franklin Watts, 2022)

Websites

Learn more about the rock cycle: www.ducksters.com/science/rocks.php

Look at diagrams and find out more about the rock cycle: www.kids.britannica.com/kids/article/rock/404136

Learn more about different kinds of rocks and the rock cycle: www.online.kidsdiscover.com/unit/geology/video/the-rock-cycle